Love Love to Love

Poetry on the spiritual transcendence
of the noun and the verb LOVE

by

Joe Bisicchia

Acknowledgements

"Timbuktu" – published by Coldnoon Diaries, 2017

"Love Is Patient, Love Is Kind" – published by Glass: Facets of Poetry, 2017

"Los Angeles" – published by The Concrete Desert Review, 2020

"New York Ever New" – published by Wingless Dreamer Publisher, 2021

"Love Is" – published by Story Embers, 2022

Contents

Love Love

Life
is a love story.

At the heart, Love.

Beyond all time and space,
yet near as the heart.

God is Love.

Not to be didactic,
but my advice is
just let go to the Word.

From before time,
the Word.
Much more than just a noun,
but a calling to all of us.

Love the noun.
And in doing so,
love too the verb.
Allow life to abound.

Without Love,
nothing exists.

With Love,
the world goes round.

There is not much more
to say about this.
Except, to love.
That's it.

And reliably,
the poetry just begins.

More than What Turns

The characters break and run
in letters to a swirl and twist
and turn with all the symbols
of the world. So much so that
all the lines, all the lengths, all
the curves, fonts, dimensions,
all the turns, all the attempted
related words, all from near
and far, all of them no longer
matter compared to the core.

What remains is ever clear.

Together, all the fractions,
all that has broken apart,
all that has opened like a
seed to be, all reveals what
simply is underneath, free
and unique, and it turns earth
its whole whirl.

There is all creation, ever
new, ever glorious, as if
by call, one heart, all, is
within the word. Love.

365

Word of the day:

Love.

Too little said?

Not enough room
to say it any less.

Etymology of Love

Love is a word, but far more than a word.

More than any alphabet.

The Word has breathed long before stripes,
long before curves and marks and runes
and will dance
long after world war fights, daggers, ruins.

Love is the Word Incarnate.

There is so much to know of the Good Lord.
Infinity wraps up in the one word.
And in it eternally dwells the ongoing plan
of every you and me, woven together,
fashioned by unfathomable hopes and dreams
to make us free. And not far apart.

With Love to dwell within our very hearts.

The Word Love

In the beginning
was the Word.

It is from which
life exists.

It is where eternity is.
It is the present.

God is

Love.

Love Is

Love begins and never ends.
Love is, with justice never distant,
raveled and unraveled, here, everywhere.

No departed utterance,
it endures beyond sounds
of rhyme, time, upon lips, here and above,
for though it always was, it always will be,
far beyond death into infinity.

In our midst, simple as this—
           Love is ubiquitous.
Nothing matters more than this—
           Love.
Was. Will be. Is. Who God is.

The Logic

Perhaps it is all illogical
for those not in love with Love.
Much depends upon us, our belief.

So goes our priceless gift of being free.
To love.

Even if setting aside any religiousness,
Love is the stuff of preciousness,
all that we can choose to revere
as highest presence.

God equals Love in that math.

And we are part of that math,
in that we are from and made to become
the embodiment of that Love,
if we believe.

And so the more we love Love,
then the more we love God.
And the more we love God,
the more we love others, and ourselves.

For some, perhaps, simple to brush it off,
to think God could never even exist,
let alone be Love.

And in a world of great need

where hunger and poverty overwhelm,
where hatred and war pull the world apart,
where communion with kindness dwindles
in shallow hearts,
perhaps it is all illogical indeed
how Love could even rise to be.

But, no matter what our choice shall be
in this world of great need for it,
Love is ever near in all its majesty,
here in all its history and manifestation,
ever reaching, ever at the ready to be new,
in every you and me.

The Meaning of Life

Here is our world, all its parade and joy,
all its color and charade. Far more than
any fleeting comfort felt, there is always more
than earth alone or stars could ever muster.
Simply power of all the universe is here,
and always was and will be our primary need.
Love.

We went metamorphosing stone into metal
into parchment circled with royal countenance,
then into plastic for subsequent acquisition
of ticket for admittance, too often bought
by theft of war, loss of freedom and soon
the bloom of personal popcorn so to escape
and fill our bellies, only to soon need refill.

Too often we lose our way in the pained race
to witness a spectacle, only to blind ourselves
to questions of all the prehistoric nothingness
that once was so long ago, now forgotten,
what was and is still an everyday miracle.
The ability to know Love.

The world shall turn and upon the strands
of every bridge, everyday things are this,
in love letters across every kitchen fridge,
we all delight in the wonder of all our gifts.
And we might realize Love patiently awaits
us with hands outstretched, and simply is.

The meaning of life is this—
the precious ability to allow Love to be
what it is.

The everyday miracle.

Circus Is in Town

Back before the sun and moon
and earth swung trapeze
here to there, and the seas swelled
pulling tributaries, back before
places were made, and faces,
back before fossils became fuel,
and asphalt became ways, and
rags became flags and became kites,
and whatever personal performance
known as daily labor became
its myriad turning of spades and
moving mud, drudgery into pitching
of masts mushrooming a big top,
and joy of that very purpose too,
whatever the particular vocation,
if only fairly paid to settle supper
onto plates, intertwined with, but
even more than any basic necessity,
if only such a human dignity,
too far often a rarity in our lack
of love and instead our slavery
to hate, we all just desperately
needed Love. Love. Simply Love.

And from heart to heart,
all of us together in turn
for this to discover—the wonder
of heaven on earth when we love
one another simple as here, now,

as an open ticket so close
to clowns with frowns.
So much awaits us under each mask
for all to share a real smile,
a real face.

And we can find the room here
in this cramped and crowded,
mystical place. For look and see,
up there above, we all can marvel
as angels leap wing to wing by faith.

More than End to End

By the grace of God,
we move and have our being.

And no matter the place,
the grace has no limit.

Simply put,
Love is where there are angels,
and we all are.

Everywhere.

Los Angeles

Gust at our backs, the constant freeway. Behind me now, some kind of unseen night bug rattling its wings or gears or others things, a bike simply faceless as it passes by me on the sidewalk, on its way. Storefront glass to storefront glass.

We are all on our way like the wind.

A weed lifts its flower bending through a Goodyear settled by my feet as I breeze on by. The world is a weed as I breathe. The world is loveliness, and I am. Settled at my feet things fall upon hell, heavenly. And dash apart like leaves only to intermingle maybe by necessity.

By the desert, and all the heat of this city street, we intertwine a fragrant aroma that moves. And stays right here by the mirroring windows of a bike store.

I see you by the storefront glass. You lay down wanting to die upon your worn bench by the bus sign, only to fall asleep and likely dream of scattered things. And I see the angels gently place by your shut face a warm bread of sorts baked on hot coals, a packaged and wrapped convenience store cake, and a can of lemonade with some percentage of fruit. After all, they know you need to eat. For the journey is a raging fire on its way here to where we currently remain, this paradise, this meandering way, this shared place of aforementioned angels.

See, yes, my bike has wings upon this worn bench. Yes, I dream of scattered things. I see me. In the storefront glass. I take my cake and drink my lemonade. The world is loveliness, and I am.

Big Word

Love
is not fanaticism of one side
pontificating font of what is right
nor self-loathing
masquerading ourselves
without punctuation the word
as fallen stardust in dying ember

Love is what it is as action
enormous in its never-ending truth
powerful in the way it is gentle
and revealing face to face

sorry to say we may not yet see it
ever near us
we too often fray blind
under a big top tarp woven tight
and evil has its ring in our circus
we may believe we are bigger things
bigger than even the wide elephants
misconstruing all our tamed beasts
loving not even ourselves tamed
resolving to be narrow
not knowing so much in names
not knowing Love in the least
losing ourselves by losing others
not loving Love in its bigness
nothing big about our bigotry
except instead ignorance

so very big and devastating
in a small mind and multiplied

sorry to say we may not yet see
in the expansive sky
all the spectrum wide light
all that we can lovingly be
when instead hiding ourselves
and all our resplendent world
in the immense darkness

Ever Near

No matter how far, Judas, show us Love.
No matter how unworthy we are, show us Love.
You know where to be, here, and let us see it here.
Let us see this, not just above, but here as Love.

Know this, Judas, here, for you are so near.
You know where to be so to unveil for us Love.
There is more to it, Judas, than a noose.
More to it than a lie of night, a feigning of it.

Do this, Judas. We know it surely means mercy.
Kiss Truth, Judas, and we shall know it to be Love.
More than a kiss, far more than an empty gesture,
but the giving of very self, the loving of Love.

Oh, too for all us,
beyond what people and history might judge,
that we may recognize and not fear it,
being ever so near it, so to be loving of Love.

Oh, Judas, do you not know Love?

Boxes

We are too quick to judge.
That is not what Love does.

Box me up and wrap the bow.
To you, I'll do the same;
I've got you all categorized now.
And same for me by you.

But what do we really know,
both of us so very clammed?

Boxes, boxes, the world abounds.
Such packaging is quite something,
something all of us are quick to do.

Crammed, slammed, jammed.
Too quickly damned.

Hurry, hurry.
Till day we are dead and buried.

One Box of Crowns

And all the world is worn.

It can be imbued
as otherworldly, pure as kindness
ever close.

All the world can be simply drawn.
Elaborately.
Wide, or stick figured too.

All the colors and their names
proliferate.
It is a big box from which to choose.

Sad, the unused.

Maybe, soon,
we all shall see each soul
in awe colors all. Each lovely too.

We could be children, new,
dreaming of sustenance and hue.

How small that way may we grow?

In Concert

Horn breathes
all lungs, speaks
all tongues.

And so it goes,
even every riotous day.

No loss in individual sound.
It remains.

We might simply listen,
in between the silence,
to all the good we are.

Our ability,
if only we should want,
for harmony
is our speaking of Love.
And defining it by what we do.

How to Pronounce Peace

Open the heart, the ears,
the discourse.
By grace, welcome the chords.
And then let go.

Like a sonic boom, yet
soft as static of a butterfly's flight.

Treasure trust in the shared song.

This is peace.

Love.
That is the phonetic way to say it.

Peace of Heaven

The world has its limits.
The heart should not.
It stays with us no matter where we are.

The city has its fossils settled,
and unsettled again by passing footsteps,
and all the past.

We lose the sun time and time again
over the high wire and trees.
Over the hill of concrete, gone.

Even in the limits here, we find our peace.
It finds us. And we share it with the world.
It begins, and begins again.

For here we are where Love has no bounds.
And of this very Love, we are
as it is in heaven,

nowhere more at home than at the heart.

Peace's Adhesiveness

Even here on the inside wall of a heart,
if only indeed it could stick more than spit,
more than noodles that tend to drip,
more than a loose brick or faded lipstick,
more than graffiti so hard to figure it.

It is simple.

It is not like any slippery healing pill
now fumbled somewhere unknown.

It is always somewhere known.

It is a lullaby
buffed smooth by a loving mother's voice.

That is the easiness in the adhesiveness of it.

Love is in its mix.

Easy for a child to see forever,
even when falling fast asleep.

Eyes Wide

With childlike minds,
sky ever blue,
what shall we innocently see?

Let us narrow not our dreams.

What might fly?

May we grow up
knowing somewhere up there
streams of love

here at ground zero as well.

But what of days
so very difficult upward to see?

Is reality farfetched as it seems.
Let us numb not the nodes
to the phenomena.

Do our prayers reach only as high
as our hearts?

Of our hearts, then,
of what are they to be?

Lift them. Together.

Who shall we see?

The Divine

Love is sacred.
Ever gentle, it goes broad-shouldered.
Moves the stars across the sky.

All powerful, it offers itself tender.
Such intimacy breathes a humanity
hallowed, filled with more than earth.
Speaks a divine tongue, yet ordinary.

It is not the obsession of possession,
but found in the giving away.
In that way, it is never self-seeking.

Love is believing all this as holy.
As seen everywhere as a sacrament
in an everyday way to be lived.

Yes, Love is meant to give.
We can choose to give ourselves to it.
And to do this, Who shall we love?
Who shall we love over everything?

The Sacred Heart.
Not just the image and likeness,
but the very Heart of Love.

Believing in Love

We can fashion facsimile gods
to fit and fill our own personal needs.
Thinking of what we supposedly love.
Flawed, those gods all fall.

Meanwhile,

beyond comprehensibility of it all,
the pained, bloodied, fallen original
with loving arms opened wide,

and with ultimate sacrifice,

still patiently, ceaselessly believes
in us,
in the Love we are fashioned to be.

May I Sing Alleluia

Oh, Mother, may I,
may I always believe.

May I always believe
in Love.

May I see Love
all around me.
And in me. Through me.

I love how you show me.
May I that way sing.
As meant to be.
Joyous and enduring.

As Love.

I love knowing that presence
as now and forever,
as if the canticle of angels
here from above, you and
they all sing along with me.

I love knowing
that the opposite of Love
may never overwhelm.

I love knowing
nothing is more powerful
than Love.

I love knowing
because I love in you
all that is Love.

Oh, Mother, full of grace,
may I,
may I sing of Love.

May I also be.

Opportunities

Cresting like waves constant to the shore,
times arrive and go, frighten and amaze,
with so many needs, and hurdles to cope.
So goes hope.
Opportunities, again, again, and again.

To love.

More than Fantasy

Hope is an endangered species.

It is crowned with a horn spiraling to heaven.
But, unlike the unicorn, will it always live
as it always did?

Yes, for it knows that Love bequeaths life.

It is why Hope twines with all that is wise.
When declared dead, inevitably,
it lifts its lovely head.

As for us,
we reach for this wished beast in the dark,
deep within the carousel of our hearts.

And, in all our limits, if wise we soon know.

Only kindness,
only Love
brings it breath.

And God is that Love.

Grace and Hope and Joy

Amazing all that fits
in a seed for a sunflower to be.
Wider than the universe.
Love takes place.

Winter may seem to have its way.
But all is melted away.
Souls never melt.
Grace is in place.

Hope knows every faraway space.
Settles home.
Always home.
Sure as a bud above the cold earth.

Joy is everywhere to the eye.
Ready as a mirror face to face.
And, as such, is like the sun.
Beaming.

For Love is what Love is.
Not to be contained.
Amazing all that fits in a heart.
And blooms.

Impact

hollow heart
goes the hater

tears apart petals

this heart so far-flung
so alone

but no one is alone

there is the universe
in each heart
we cradle it and dream
what might become
what shall ignite
what shall spread
far-flung

if only Love

if only the seed
to bloom ribbons
on a rose
beyond the thorns

Loves Me Knot

A heart can hurt,
probably like a flower
when its petals are pulled off.

What matters is within.
Always at the ready to begin.

I hope I'll have survivability,
this heart by spring,
enduring as the present,
wrapped in a bow,

enough to find
in the dead branches of nothing
everything.

Our Petals Fall

Too often, goes dim our dirt below,
the bloodshed has spread,
and we plant emblems instead.

Our world turns, and it turns.
And what goes green goes red.
We hurt.

We circle time and time again.
We lose faith that Love does as well,
in the ongoing crown of thorns.

So much of Love we easily forget.

In our ignorance, we don't realize it,
even then, just how much we miss
overstepping the fallen road signs
along the way.

Driving Hazard

Narcissus me,
I may love that mirror
so to see me.

But,
I can be
so inflated
    I cannot see.

Like driving a car
full of balloons.

Too much goes
unseen,
trapped in own skin,
human race
in solitary seat
and annoyed.

Air bag

soon to be deployed.

Sign of Indifference

On the pedestal, these words appear:
REST IN PEACE.

That said, now I dig deep,
wondering what those words really mean.

Meanwhile, where is peace
when geese freely release at my feet
while I break down piece by piece?

LOOK ON MY WORKS, YE MIGHTY,
AND DESPAIR!

Yes, to worship oneself—
so it goes to live under a tyrant.

And that's me.

But the geese apparently can't read.

And unless nearby Mary still prays for me
now and at the hour of my death,
I guess the world will always mourn me
as it mourns the passing of winter.

One might think I'm dead
just like all the rest.
Maybe I'm just a cemetery worker

digging graves and lining the engraved.
Whining over geese.

I know I am in the dark not knowing Love.
I don't care much anymore.
Things I used to love have become dust.
What's the opposite of love?
Well, one might simply think it is to hate.
I sure do some of that, but this I know—
now being numb might be even less fun.
And less peace.

this is hell

numb

we've lost our hearts

selves

torn apart

sun rises

we remain

the dead of night

hell on a pedestal

Yes, we appreciate art.
And yes,
we may be biased
toward beautiful things.

But,
after a while,
sure seems that hell
in all its fanciful poses
with hatred underneath
is just smack dab ugly.

Yet another reason
to collect love over hate
in our everyday gallery.

Lost in Selfishness

What I remember most of the day I drove to hell was the emptiness of worshiping only myself. Saw Satan while I was there. We shared the rearview mirror and saw nothing.

Wonder if maybe Satan is erased as only immortally human, but now devoured of the power of infinite divinity, the power namely the ability to love simply, eternally. Maybe the devil himself or herself is then lost in the never-ending finite, in all that human insecurity, all that loneliness, all that emptiness accrued in selfishness.

That inability to love is what I remember most about hell. Love forgotten in the colossal loss of one's self. All that depth of true love, not known.

No love.

I move on for I only know so much. Enough to know how simple it is to define the inability to love.

no exile

can there be
banishment from Love?
I can rush inside
to emptiness I can rush
inside to recidivism
a cage to escape
time can stop still
time flies
here outside paradise
confined and paralyzed
running hamster wheel
by hate
as if only to hell
the loveless place

instead
if only no gate
instead to vastness
to fly free by mercy
grace
to rush inside
to fullness to rush
timeless
inside outside
where there is Love
help me to help me
again
by Love
help me to love

New York Ever New

Dr. King spoke of hate,
and the only way
out of its darkness.

See us, persistent pillars,
you standing aside me
connected in grace.

See us everywhere,
even in the shattered rubble
where love is all that is left.

See today, vault of heaven
as it still shimmers the glass.
You, my neighbor,

we share a face.
Hate has countless separate faces.
Love has just one.

We stand in all its light.

To Make a Stand

Surrender.

Fall

in love
with what is right

         so to stand up
            for it.

Roots to sky.

Love
reveals its bearing
in its engineering.

Same as Here

Somewhere
sky may be green,
purple may be the sea,
and snow tangerine.
There it may be as always was.

But such will be no fuss for us
if indeed there too can be Love.
We can be at home
there same as here
despite disparate trivialities.

Good thing God knows
no boundaries.

Our Flag

At times ignited by the ignorant
for their cause with fire at ours,
desired ember to them, but colors remain.

Indelible, the ideal.

Shame if any colors are not plain,
if they fail to unveil humankind's domain
to dream a dream shared—
     Freedom,
          ours and for others everywhere.
Even for those sadly unaware.

Whatever the cloth, it should represent the ideal,
but the template is the ideal.

And it is made to be real.

In gallant waves proudly for all those who dare
with fire in their beings to die for it,
not so much for an individual flag that is visible,
but for God-given dignity under the same God
indivisible.

Such is the stuff of love.

That is the glory, the flame inextinguishable.

All Flags

In the shared pain divisive,
we made our snow angels,
our Malmedy Massacre.
White became red.
Sad how in the numb air
so much innocence just melts away.

Freedom calls for us to listen.
Bang drums for war, but be wary
our souls may deafen.

Instead, somehow,
may our rhythm, our love, outlive the pain.

So many open their hearts for such freedom.

Skin lies empty, bodies of work
open on the field, sacrificed.
Each no longer cries,
for each is now only earth.
Remains still. Side by side. Heroes.
  And see, another soul flies.

O, say can you hear?

Percussion of a nation,
like fireworks in the distance,
a clapping child wearing mittens.

All flags flap like that.

Woven

Of what is my knot,
my embrace,
my silk?

How tight am I wound?
Can I bend in the wind?
Will I break apart?

How may I be of the breeze,
its very color?
Let me be such.

Let me be me.
All my pain,
my loss,
my victory.

Let me rise again.
Never alone
but in a line of flagpoles,
the sky shared.

Together, let us stand
for what is loving and free,
and that way be
equally compared.

Love Is Free

Love is
such a lofty word of Higher Things.
And yet, down to earth.
Priceless, yet indeed free.
The choice to love is personal.
For some, conditional.
Conditional love is far incomplete.

For Love, it is unconditional.

In Who should you trust for this to be?

If you do not believe in Love,
you still breathe and have ability to be free.

Yet, no matter what you do,
will Love believe in you?

It is a question posed to every me.

Maybe, from somewhere it is just a gift,
the knowledge of all that is,
to comprehend the freedom to even dismiss this
as an inane question lost in a false premise.

Maybe the gift comes from Love.
Simple and sincere. As a child.
As a life amongst us all, to freely live.

Some things are so hard to comprehend.
In the end, some things are easy to comprehend
as a gift given
and a gift to give.

Love Is Never a Limited Offer

So much goodness in store.
Not at the store around the block.
Can't buy Love in any store.
But, always plenty in stock,
close by,
on the shelves of the heart.
And it's free!
We can share it with the world.
Come back for more.
Open round the clock.

Love Forever Widens

Frame it not as if in a birdcage,
contained.
It needs to fly free.
Never confined within a circle,
it circles.
Open wide your wings.

Love has no limit.

Allow your heart to be.

Infinite.

Human Sized Heart

Treasures
will never please those
who always want more.
To those unfortunate minds,
acquired desires will fade
in dreams for bigger designs.

Lost love falls behind in gems
never to be realized.
And all the while,
never attained is peace
of being truly satisfied.

Yet, for those of true happiness,
of blessed richness,
every day of growing gratifies
a human sized heart.
For them, the natural *now*
fits squarely
in its supernatural dimensions.

Made to love.

Be Lovable

There is space.
It awaits for you to be available.
To fill it in with grace.
And simply be LVABL.

Despite what goes missing,
ever remains the meaning.
And it's believable.
Let it be.

Corpus Christi

And daily as heaven descends, and ascends,
and somehow remains, we go this way ever still,
peace of a verdant field with our shepherd.

And so it goes, despite all the arrows,
and it grows despite desperate desert of stone and tar.
What rushes, rushes, awaits. What hurts and celebrates
is simply life.

This is our earthen way. It springs forth as we go free,
sits ever still upon a shared liberty, cries upon the pain
of ignorance, numbed, yet again new and begun, stings,
but also comforts as we, in the image and likeness
of Love take joy in the splendid way of the good Lord.

Here I meet you, just a stranger on the way.
We soon realize we know each other from forever.
We recognize ourselves in each other's eyes.

Love's Nationality

Divine, the template,
we come in assorted sizes, colors,
and yet, not so very far in the face.

So goes Love.

Love does not separate place from place.
It knows no borders.

It knows no end.

Welcomed within, let Love be.

God is Love.

Never far, but close at heart.

So then, in the mirror, and in a stranger,
and in a friend,

Who do you see?

Standard Time

Clocks may differ
but now
is always the same.

How very far are you
from me?

Do we both not breathe?

There is a presence
to this present.

How shall we allow it
to be?

Momentary Peace in War

beyond time
and space

under heavy stars
dreaming of back yards

ever awake
the heart can break

but never go empty
Love is never empty

mothers and children embrace
heart to heart

here
no matter how far apart

one precious moment
though a world away

one immeasurable swirl
ever still

believing
what is

no distance
no wall

no force can separate
heart to heart

To Become Love

Indeed love Love.

Become that way full.

For, in the words of Saint Clare:
"We become what we love
and who we love shapes
what we become.

If we love things,
we become a thing.

If we love nothing,
we become nothing."

Nothing
is emptier than nothing.

When Love Is Encased in Ice

Inside, what shall prove to be?

If only we shall breathe
and be free each to be as made to be.
Each one of a kind, never alone.

Underneath, in the melting,
we just might find the realness
beyond defining.

After all the evaporating, together,
radiating what is within outward,
let it be simply divining.

The air we breathe.

Missing What Matters

When love is missed
and now thought lost,
how sad it wasn't found
all along.

For, by mercy, it still is.

Love is always present.

Beyond one's joy,
beyond one's pain,
beyond one's self, it is.

Never Truly Lost

There is a phantom
to the faraway place
to tomorrow,
to today,
as each moment by moment
seems to say turn away.

But moment by
moment by moment
is opportunity

if one allows it.

For Love to find a way.

Break of a Lifetime

We are all broken apart.

But, even when all is doom,
and most especially then,
Love makes room.
Ever filling us.

Ever reaching,
ever pulling us together.

God is love.

The Cross is the proof.

In Him we intersect.
In Him we unite, as new.
Overflowing.

small world

Betcha ten bucks to Timbuktu,
you have your big old dreams
like I do too.

You've visited forever,
and played checkers there too.

It's not a billion light years away,
not too far away to see.

It's all inside your face,
nudged next to your big old dreams.
Seems so much space inside a face
to leave as an empty place.

So, when you smile,
sky blooms the sun anew.
Lights up everyone.
How can it not?
You have your small world
like I do too.

Timbuktu

What does Timbuktu mean to you?
Is it a tired cliché of somewhere far, far away?
Is it like nothing you know, just plain peculiar,
something to ignore?
Is it foreign and unfamiliar
and thus such a strange and dangerous place?
Would it be dreadful being there
having to wear a stranger's face?
Is it far as the world,
distant as the dark outside your door?
Is it safely fictitious, a place too far-flung,
too make-believe, too much like Loch Ness,
too unknown to even be true?
Or, is it too real, and thus a sensible feel
of a place to stay away from?

But, what if you must surrender to trust
and yield to what is ultimately real,
would you be comfortable
using what your gifts were given for?
What if there in Timbuktu,
it's there where your leap of faith has taken you?
What would you find so very regular
and so very new?
Would the dramatic or anticlimactic unearthing
be vicious or serendipitous?

Caution may very well suit you in Timbuktu
and everywhere.

A den of cubs especially is personal to a mother bear.
Your haven is something rather exclusive to you too.

Yet, just as you are never too far from home
to write a poem,
and never too far to get on your knees to pray,
you are never too far to communicate in a human way.
Safe to say, if you can behold true gold in others
and in you,
you might just feel at home even in Timbuktu.

Philadelphia

Wrapped in your meaning, find love.
So much burdens the world in hate,
but let us each be brave to love anyways.

Make it enduring love, surely big as a city,
but borrow it not as a proper noun.
Make it a loanword.
Fashion it common abstract
and make it zeitgeist for anywhere.

From here in a city named after that love,
let us hold truths to be self-evident,
that all are created equal,
and may we take this around the world
to each, and each, and each of the created,
for each is endowed by their Creator
with certain unalienable Rights,
that among these are Life, Liberty and
the pursuit of Happiness.

Yet, don't complicate it.

It is not that big a word, even though
it is indeed broad as it comes to being.
Give it sustainability beyond language.

Let is speak via the heart
with gentle, kind, inspiring action
and carry it wherever you are.

Be willing to give it away.

And have it come back to you,
not just brotherly, but sisterly too,
no matter the place.

And let its meaning never be lost.
So goes Love, as Love is wont to do.

Home with Many Rooms

There is a place that just is.
Simple as here
and just as intricate.
More than the universe.
Pure as Love is.

There is a time that just is
as it is,
with all the past
and all the future within.
Just is, as is.

There is a way that just is.
With us.
Within.
For as I Am always is,
thus we all are.

For in that Heart all is
home.

Where There Is Love

There is room.
For family, friends,
for strangers,
there is room.

So, awaken the verb.
Go and love.
Sow love.
Love big.

For there is room.

Seeds bend and break,
and life is to begin again.
Even if thought forgotten,
somewhere always home.

Near as here
even at supper table,
our hearts ever able
to give of ourselves.

Full of bloom.

Largesse

Let us overlook the distance,
the wide expanse,
you to me, me to you,
the vast space in this, our view
to heaven, big as every soul.

There is the universe
in every soul, hard to hold.
So much is given by the Giver.
When grace overflows,
kindness knows no measure.

How big is it to love
when all along
Love is here,
big as the universe?
See how Love is big enough.

Selfless

Unkind
the temporal world
as we know it.
Cruel, the survival
of the fittest,
the dog-eat-dog of it.

Yet,
what bridges the finite
beyond time?

Love.

Love is all-in.
Willing to sacrifice
even all esteem.
True leaders selflessly lead
even if it means in retreat.

We all must know when
to surrender, so to win.
Even in the deepest division,
and most especially then,
there is Love.

And in surrendering to it,
see the glory in self.

The Inner Voice

Listen.
Like Helen Keller to water.
Even in the blind silence. So goes Love.

Speak.
Be open to the poetry within, but share it.
Be it. So goes Love.

More than mouth and ear.
More than just a feeling or desire.
We are an active spirit. So goes Love.

Mortal, we need.
We are more than mortal.
And, by Love, we shall not want.

If only we finally realize who we are within,
all intertwined, made of the stuff ever Divine,
connected to all that moves the cosmos.

Person by person by irreplaceable person
created, we are one and ever new.
So goes Love.

Another Baby Is Born

All of us, each of us,
amen, my friend, again we begin.
Despite all that ends, Love always begins.

And her tapestry is here in Jersey City
in the neighborhood she shall live,
a togetherness now knit wide to the world.

Warmth of a shared home everyone weaves.
Please let her breathe, for she is all of life.
Amen, my friend, again we begin.

More than just another place, this swath,
face to face to face, only all of Eden.
And the sowing is in this and every place.

And yet another baby everywhere is born.
Despite all that ends, Love always begins.
Despite all that ends, Love always begins.

Extra Chromosome

Child, you show it, and we all can.
Through Love, hope for our planet is planted.
We are all such children.

Through Love,
even that which is deemed imperfect by others,
has a way of no mistake.

You show it, that we all can be it.
Extra.
For with you, the world is extraordinary.

Through Love.

Unfathomable Force

Love is.
Too immense to measure.
Yet simple in an everyday way.
It compacts all the universe in a seed, and
tosses upward a confetti of stars, and
all the moments of all our lives, and
rolls the skies, and turns the sun, and
pulls the daisy so to go face to face
with a marveling child.

Obit of a Philanthropist

Meanwhile,
an old kind woman has died.
The poor and the homeless
know this.

She has died.
Survived by all of us.

We have cried.

And rolled up our sleeves.
For she taught us
we all travel time.
To now.
To savor all of life.

She taught us.
To give.

Of ourselves.

And in that way receive.

For Love gives.

Loves gives and gives.

What Is Needed

So much to do.
There is so much good needed to be done.

There is such a void in what is left undone.
Rather than avoiding it,
and rather than being apart,
be a part of the do.

What is simply needed is you.

To Have and to Hold

Remember, we had dug up a thesaurus
in the park, its old bones sticking out
from leathered skin, a long grounded
winged creature. You held it and labored
to find the word of the shape we were in.
Looked for a synonymous definition.

Not a dead word or thing of the past.
Maybe misused, worn, hidden, forgotten.
But a word waiting for another chance.

To have purpose.

You found it.
Or the archaeology of forever found us,
uncovered for itself in its own time now
just how it is we get by.

And every day onward from then, same.
We never looked for a better word
narrowing down our everyday devotion.
Love has a beautiful name.

Valentine

Long after Eden, but of heaven here,
before rigor mortis of the heart, we love
all that our Love is, even the biting cold,
the far off spring and the standing rose twigs.
And the church to be found on Whitefriar Street
where blooms wait to abound, and here
where turns our soil in patches of our own,
best when earth is open, rather than closed.

We have had our wounds, and endless mercy.
Our lives are made of selfless love,
far more that what drifts as ghosts.
And our recent trash bag wafts by a window
and we follow to the other window out back,
and watch it grab onto a winter thorn,
and wonder of our own eventual reliquary
amidst this garden where roses will be ready

by the banging trashcans, as all the world
twists all our soon to be strewn pains
into the wind.

And we smile for each other.
Love, even if seemingly imperfect,
is perfect, and somehow always begins.

Stronger than Death

Love is.

More than we can make.
Despite all that complicates.

Waits in its truest form
forever, and never breaks.

Even amidst the sadness,
goes ultimate joy.

For Love never ends
but forever begins again.

For Love is
God.

I Still Remember

Yes, I still remember the love. I remember the love, yes, despite the pain of that resplendent autumn day, ever wide, the burn at my neck when they killed me in their ignorance. I remember the love.

Before that day, before that loveless age, there was a time of innocence. There was a time
we ran through the field and chased the butterflies. There was a time we were just children, growing too fast. Children, yes. Equality with God, I cannot grasp. Can I forgive and forget?

Who am I to judge? Of love, I pray I may be the river and be as I am and allow forgetfulness to be a way of…whatever.

I forget the bite at my neck, the tingling, strangling. Instead, I remember sun's crystals dancing upon the river that dazzling autumn day when they killed me in their blind rage. There was a flush of colors unafraid in the leaves, an intelligence to me of what shall not pass. Like all, I am made of such love, I am, by an unending force from above, made to last.

And maybe, maybe in all of us, so much of that is far too easy to forget.

There was a time maybe we knew what love was, so to remember. Somewhere I had heard the rush, the hollering of men. I prayed for mercy for them and for me, that maybe, maybe when awake, by grace, if anything, rather than hate, it would be love, yes, it would love that was remembered, enough to start an elegy somewhere written on a distant page, yet near the heart, a part of all that is and was, and shall forever be the gift from above.

Terms & Conditions

Small, we share the road. Enemy, be as you are,
and same for me.

I shall trust in what remains the same,
that which has no end. I shall love.

Often I've lied.
I wanted so much.

What goes limitless lets go, goes unconditional,
goes merciful in my imperfection, goes boundless.

I shall still love you and thus see God.
Therein, my strength. Therein, my peace.

Therein, by grace, both our victory.

Heaven's Rain

Love gathers.

How far down can it reach?
Upon the roofs of our homes?

Can Love's falling go further deep,

fill our hearts,

and settle in our bones?

Love gathers.

See how the Sower waits
for the precious fruit of the earth,
being patient with it.

For it to be more than just a word.
For it to be the verb.

Let it be.

Desert and parched land will exult;
the steppe will rejoice and bloom.

Heaven is no longer concealed.

Love gathers.

And our souls shall be healed.

Today's Forecast

And so the fallen leaves are like crabs
scampering down the glistening street.
Soon to lay down their arms and stick.
Trees no longer unravel a tarp
above our shanty, our shingles in disarray.
And cold wind cuts through the bones
under our hard to hold down lids.

And, yet,
we can almost see the polka dot rain
as it sings atop our flat roof to accumulate
like good deeds upon us.
Each prism is like everyone we meet
for we are so far from alone, to be reached.
Let the sky pour like poems
upon all peoples, as if beyond time,
as if fallen

upon us and lined with purpose
as if we were in mind ages before the sun
to precipitate and to invigorate
and like water to bless the land again and
to evaporate yet again, and ages hence
again, again, again to run like rain
through our beating hearts.

So goes kindness in the shape of love.
For all of us in this shared place known as
everywhere,
this is the blessed shape we are in.
Let it rain.

Even If Memory Shall Fade

Love is a permanent place.
Its field of green bends to the sun.
It does not fade or go away.
A dream can dissipate.
Better to have a dream than not.
A dream is twined with hope.
Such is the stuff that trails the skies,
at times thought untouchable above,
but runs through our hearts
here where we are, through Love.

To be alive, we shall love.

We shall open our eyes.

We shall close our eyes.

We all shall die.

But Love somewhere saves each face.
See the sunset Love hath made.
Even as the sun somewhere hides.

And Love outlasts the sun.

Near as Now

Love is.

We can go always waiting
for Love to begin.
Our opportunities often end
without even the noticing.

But here we are again.

The present in a bow.

And under a delicious sun,
plans spread before us,
all our assorted hopes,
all our tasks and troubles,
our dreams for this day.

And we can choose Love.

It is how everything falls
into place.

Love is Patient, Love is Kind

We've walked.
And I forget we've walked on water.

You've fed the multitude, raised the dead
and I forget.

We've talked
and I've forgotten what you've said.

And yet,
you reach out your hand

and we walk.

The Next Step

And now, there is heaven in the distance.
Its spires rise in the haze.
I move along toward the shared bridge.

It shall be a mirage. I think.
All shall soon become familiar.
As I get near, heaven is indeed here.
As it is. As all along the everyday way.
I share this road of the Samaritan.
Signs again arrive. Just ahead. One by one.

Shape up, here comes the way of Love.
Yes, Love. Yes, yet another chance.

Beyond any fleeting word,
Who shall I dare to see?
The robber, the victim, the neighbor,
the passerby?

And who shall I prove to truly be?
Who looks for me now in the face?

Love

I Am
Who Am.
More than words.
The Word.
Love.

Welcome every moment
as new.
Ages to ages to now.
All along,
make My heart your home.

This day and every day
and in all I ever create
see also you.
Love.

Now, go and do.

www.ingramcontent.com/pod-product-compliance
Lightning Source LLC
LaVergne TN
LVHW090117180726
843489LV00002B/863